The Complete
Concordance
to Aleister Crowley's
The Book of the Law
(Liber AL vel Legis)

Compiled by Wolgang Gregory Zeuner

Fenris Brothers
an imprint of the
Crossquarter Publishing Group
PO Box 8756
Santa Fe, NM 87504
(505) 438-9846 voice/fax

The Complete **Concordance**
to Aleister Crowley's
The Book of the Law (Liber AL vel Legis)

Dedications

I dedicate this book to the people who most inspired its creation and long-delayed publication:

- skeptical students of Aleister Crowley;
- Jay William Koelsch and Caroline Heffernan, my fellow errant students of the High Arts;
- and most especially, my children, Inanna Leigh and Graeme Anthony, ever and always.

Compiler's Note

The Book of the Law was produced in three sections; the following study will notate them as I, II, and III. These correspond to the pagination of the 1938 OTO edition (the standard version) thus: I, pp 19-28; II, pp 29-38; III, pp 39-49.

The notations that follow, however, ignore pagination, but are simple to read. For example, the word "joy" first appears at I,13,14, which means the first book, thirteenth section (stanza or "page" as some say), fourteenth word. The reader is on her/his own as to the precise significance, if any, of these numbers.

The notation has been reduced in a manner we find easy to use. So, the second reference for "joy" is ,,19; this means that it is in the same book and section as the immediately previous citation, and the notation in this instance is short-hand for "I,13,19". We think this is also desirable as it calls immediate attention to words that are heavily used in a few clustered areas.

Rarely, a phrase or compound has been notated as a single word; for example, "an-hungered", "star-splendoured", "Ra Hoor Khut", "718". We have tried to be consistent with this, and apologise for any disagreements. Linguistically, however, some compoundings form a distinct connotative gestalt that is far removed from the denotation of the individual pieces.

A reference number appears in parentheses when the word is part of one of these compounds, in order to call attention to its variance with the other occurrences.

Preface

In publishing this Concordance, we stand in slight violation of the Comment that completes *Liber AL*, which specifically warns against both the study and the discussion of the Book. However, though such study is indeed a constant concern of those who seek hidden, esoteric meanings in the text, we believe that such a Concordance is at least as much an aid to those who train their minds in the overt Truth as it is to those who ignore the sublimity of the obvious in search of secrets. Therefore, let it be made available to the wise and unwise alike, whether in support of meditation or obsession.

This introductory section will provide a few starting-off points for the serious researcher. They stem from basic word-frequency and pattern analyses, methods which are easy enough to master but which might only sidetrack someone who wished to concentrate on the actual study of the Book.

The first point is that the three books of *Liber AL* bear certain linguistic differences among themselves. To someone who is very familiar with the text, it is almost as if the three parts were written by different authors. This would be consistent with Crowley's assertion that he had received the books as different "transmissions". The scholar may find it enlightening to examine particular words, to see which ones are used heavily in one book, yet not at all in another – and then to search out a reason. It is to the serious student to determine which of these anomalies are significant, and why.

- no variant of "adore" appears in **II**
- "ah" appears five times, only near the end of **II**
- "art" (either meaning) is used twice in **I**, nine times in **II**, and not at all in **III**
- "aught is used exactly once in each book
- "Because", as a proper noun, six times in **II**, once in **III**
- "can" twice in **I**, once in **III**; "cannot" once in **II**, and "canst" twice
- "choose" once in each book
- "chosen" five times each in **I** and **II**
- "console", "consoled", and "consoler" once each in **II**
- "dead" twice in **II**; "death" twice in **I**, 14 times in **II**, once in **III**; "die" four times in **II**, once in **III**; "dying" once in **II**
- "Do what thou wilt" appears exactly once
- dogs are popular in **II**
- "does" and the archaic "dost" and "doth" are each used once, in **II**
- "ecstasy" is not used in **III**
- "end" once in each book
- the same is true for "Equinox"
- "every" does not appear in **III**
- "exalt" only once, in **III**, and is the only "ex-" prefix in that book
- "fall" (and "falling") once in **III**, not at all in **I**, though "fell" appears there, once
- "feast" 12 times in **II**, not at all in the others
- "find" four times in **II**
- "fool" once in each book; "fools" is not so evenly distributed

- "fresh" three times in III
- "from" five times in I, ten times in III
- "heart" appears exactly four times in each book; "hearts" is not in III
- "her" is not used at all in II
- "hidden" is once in each I and III; "hide" and "hiding" each twice in II
- "him" only once in II, though common enough in I and III
- "incense" only in I, twice
- "infinite" not in III
- "King" (proper) appears only in II, ten instances, and twice as plural
- "kiss" three times in I, "kisses" three times in II
- "knowest" once per book
- no laughs in I
- no life in III
- "lift" six times in II, once in III
- "little" five times in I, once in III
- the three Lords in III
- love decreases from one book to the next, appearing only once in III
- "more" three times, only in II
- "mysteries" once in each book
- "name" three times in each book
- "old" once in each book
- II doesn't have an ordeal
- "our" eight times, only in II
- "perfume" and "perfumes" once each in I and III
- "pride" once in each book
- "proof" four times, in III
- "rapture" six times, all in III
- "rejoice" four times, all in II
- "rich" three times in each I and III

- III has no ritual or rule
- "slay" only in III
- sorrow reigns in II
- I has all the space
- there is one star in III
- I has no strength
- "Thee" capitalised appears exactly once in each book
- so, too, for "things"
- "through" once in I, seven in III
- "To me! To me!" three times in I
- "torment", "torn", and "torture" in III, once each
- look at "true", "truly", and "truth"
- "up" ten times in II, once in III
- no "us" in III (and see "we")
- "veil" and "veiling" vs. "veiled"
- no war in II
- "way" and "ways": once each in I, three each in III
- "we" only in II, five times
- "will" is rich with meaning and variation
- "women" once in each book
- "worship" increases from book to book

The text also contains certain oddities of typography. There are no less than six variants of "Ra Hoor Khuit". Again, it is entirely to the individual scholar to make use of the fact and the reason for it.

Finally, please be reminded: the reason for such research as this current volume (and others in the future) is simply that it has not been done previously, even on a work so well-known as *Liber AL*. As an object lesson, the fruit yet to be borne by that large book should remind all serious occultists of the depths still unplumbed everywhere around.

— *Wolf Zeuner*, *2001 C.E.*

A

a   I,3,7 ,16,5 ,,9 ,22,16 ,26,26 ,27,27
,33,6 ,41,36 ,46,3 ,48,4 ,50,3 ,54,9
,56,33 ,60,18 ,,48 ,61,28 ,,39 ,,121
,,127 II,7,25 ,14,5 ,15,46 ,19,2 ,,7
,22,48 ,,59 ,24,81 ,,83 ,27,16 ,28,2
,32,4 ,,9 ,33,8 ,37,1 ,38,1 ,39,1 ,40,1
,,8 ,41,1 ,,6 ,,10 ,,15 ,42,1 ,43,1
,49,27 ,,37 ,52,3 ,53,38 ,58,61 ,,63
,,78 ,59,8 ,,18 ,61,3 ,,10 ,63,22 III,2,8
,3,10 ,7,5 ,10,49 ,11,74 ,12,7 ,24,14
,31,3 ,38,14 ,,25 ,,53 ,39,4 ,,14 ,41,5
,42,85 ,43,50 ,45,16 ,47,71 ,,81 ,49,4
,74,3.

abased   III,46,16.

abide   III,38,116; ,39,91.

Abomination of Desolation   III,19,7-9.

about   I,50,7; II,24,55; ,26,7; III,6,3; ,9,19; ,71,5.

above   I,13,3; ,14,1.

abrahadabra III,1,1.

Abrahadabra III,47,85; ,75,9.

Abramelin III,23,16.

abrogate I,49,1.

absolve I,53,39.

abstruction III,11,21.

achieve III,45,47.

accursed I,41,38; ,,39; II,29,4.

add I,25,2.

adorant I,49,45.

adorations III,38,43.

adore I,11,6; III,37,2; ,,45; ,,67.

Adorer I,21,6.

adulterous III,44,32.

aeons I,41,44.

after III,10,41; ,12,6; ,47,52; ,,98.

afterward III,23,21.

again III,20,13.

against	II,22,52; ,24,95; ,25,3; III,49,10.
agelong	II,66,45.
ah	II,66,22; ,69,1; ,,2; ,73,1; ,,2.
Ahatoor	III,38,77.
Aiwass	I,7,6.
alienate	III,43,39.
all	I,15,28; ,23,12; ,26,31; ,,33; ,27,63; ,30,21; ,31,13; ,32,24; ,,45; ,,50; ,,55; ,34,22; ,41,33; ,42,14; ,47,12; ,49,3; ,,5; ,,7; ,51,25; ,,78; ,54,19; ,56,20; ,,25; ,,49; ,,58; ,57,57; ,60,6; ,61,8; ,,56; ,,66; ,,146; ,62,2; ,,40; II,2,2; ,9,2; ,,10; ,22,45; ,,67; ,24,72; ,32,15; ,58,41; ,59,4; ,64,12; ,72,26; III,2,15; ,16,22; ,17,4; ,22,11; ,29,15; ,38,37; ,39,1; ,41,7; ,44,48; ,45,20; ,47,7; ,,65; ,49,11; ,55,12; ,57,3; ,,13; ,68,3.
alone	II,23,3; III,47,102.
aloud	II,54,6.
Alphabet	II,55,11.
already	III,10,17.
also	I,22,42; ,37,1; ,49,32; ,51,93; ,53,22; ,57,73; ,60,45; II,24,9; ,32,1; III,25,13; ,27,1; ,28,1; ,47,83; ,56,1; ,57,2.

9

altar	III,30,2.
always	I,51,112; ,61,98; III,47,10.
am	I,13,2; ,21,8; ,,22; ,22,4; ,,32; ,24,2; ,26,12; ,29,3; ,61,145; ,64,2; ,,10; II,2,16; ,,24; ,3,5; ,6,2; ,,20; ,7,2; ,,9; ,8,10; ,11,12; ,15,3; ,,20; ,,31; ,16,2; ,,2; ,22,2; ,23,2; ,,10; ,26,2; ,47,3; ,48,10; ,49,2; ,,7; ,,34; ,50,2; ,62,2; ,65,2; III,3,9; ,17,47; ,22,22; ,37,8; ,38,79; ,42,23; ,,27; ,46,2; ,49,2; ,70,2; ,72,2.
amen	II,49,19.
amn	I,51,60.
among	I,22,52; II,74,25; ,77,7; ,78,11; ,,14; III,55,18.
an [a]	I,64,7; II,49,40; III,4,3; ,21,12; ,34,23; ,61,3; ,72,29.
an [&?]	II,72,15.
and (or &)	I,3,3; ,6,9; ,9,5; ,10,6; ,,13; ,11,10; ,12,8; ,13,5; ,15,9; ,,19; ,16,7; ,,19; ,21,4; ,,24; ,,32; ,22,12; ,,35; ,,58; ,24,4; ,,9; ,25,4; ,26,5; ,,14; ,,42; ,,49; ,,60; ,27,5; ,,16; ,,55; ,28,6; ,,11; ,30,16; ,31,6; ,32,42; ,33,11; ,34,15; ,37,4; ,,8; ,,16; ,,26; ,40,25; ,,28; ,42,9; ,43,3; ,45,3; ,,9; ,48,16; ,49,9; ,,25; ,,53; ,50,18; ,,39; ,,51; ,,53; ,51,16; ,,20; ,,24; ,,29; ,,31; ,,71; ,,85; ,,89; ,,97; ,,106; ,53,13; ,,25; ,,45; ,56,24; ,,54;

,57,23; „29; „49; ,59,7; „9; ,60,23; „38;
,61,31; „74; „78; „95; „104; „124; „148;
„150; „162; ,62,11; „22; II,2,4; „27; ,4,6;
,6,12; „22; ,7,5; „15; ,9,19; ,11,7; ,13,8;
,14,16; ,15,7; „22; „36; ,16,5; ,17,11; „18;
,18,15; ,20,2; „6; „10; ,21,7; „30; „44;
„94; „105; ,22,8; „10; „13; „26; „35; „71;
,24,43; „45; „50; „75; ,26,23; „34; „44;
„46; ,27,28; ,28,5; ,30,4; „12; ,32,12;
„14; ,34,8; ,35,9; ,36,7; ,37,10; ,39,5;
,40,7; ,41,5; „14; ,43,7; ,44,13; ,48,21;
,49,4; „17; „32; ,50,4; „20; „25; ,52,23;
„56; „62; ,53,20; ,55,6; ,58,12; ,60,4; „6;
,62,7; ,63,19; ,64,33; „40; ,66,2; „8; „20;
„52; ,70,4; „32; „43; ,72,5; „11; ,74,17;
,75,6; ,77,5; ,78,41; ,79,8; „10; III,3,14;
,8,8; ,10,13; „20; ,11,49; „59; „65; ,12,4;
,14,9; ,17,45; ,18,10; ,19,14; ,21,26;
,22,35; „40; ,23,5; „7; „17; „20; „23;
,25,7; „22; „39; ,26,6; ,27,6; ,34,14; „20;
„28; „42; „49; „55; „68; „77; „95; ,35,10;
,37,13; „52; „59; ,38,8; „71; „75; ,39,3;
„13; „19; „30; „36; „53; „61; „65; ,40,10;
„19; ,41,12; ,42,18; „25; „59; „69; ,43,8;
„10; „52; „62; „65; ,44,31; „39; „42;
,45,38; ,46,14; „23; „33; „54; ,47,28;
„84; „91; ,48,9; ,52,10; ,53,12; „16; ,55,5;
,58,4; „9; ,63,9; „12; ,64,8; ,70,9; ,72,30;
,73,8; ,74,9.

an-hungered [enhungered?]   III,43,66.

animal   II,70,21.

11

Ankh-af-na-khonsu I,14,31; ,36,3; III,37,28; ,38,86.

another   II,24,93; ,,99; III,25,14; ,34,51; ,,62; ,,73;
               ,,85; ,,91; ,47,33.

answered   I,26,22; ,27,4.

any   I,22,55; ,,59; II,22,76; ,24,91; III,17,24;
               ,46,61.

anything   III,17,13.

apostle   I,15,10.

apparel   I,51,81.

appear   III,37,69.

arched   I,26,46.

ardours   I,14,19.

are   I,11,2; ,,13; ,14,28; ,17,3; ,21,16; ,31,26;
               ,40,19; ,45,6; ,,13; ,48,11; ,49,2; ,,33; ,,37;
               ,50,13; ,51,2; ,,22; ,,69; ,52,14; ,,19;
               ,56,22; ,57,21; ,57,64; ,60,10; ,,40; II,5,8;
               ,9,13; ,,20; ,15,39; ,17,13; ,18,2; ,,10; ,,22;
               ,19,13; ,20,12; ,21,98; ,24,8; ,25,2;
               ,26,26; ,,49; ,32,18; ,36,2; ,47,5; ,50,23;
               ,52,50; ,53,8; ,,23; ,54,21; ,,27; ,56,19;
               ,58,11; ,,49; ,64,6; ,66,55; ,,58; III,22,30;
               ,,38; ,37,31; ,38,41; ,46,15; ,47,36; ,58,13;
               ,68,14.

argue   III,42,37.

argument	III,11,9.
aright	I,52,5; ,57,65; II,5,31; III,10,18.
arise	III,34,41; ,,54.
armies	II,24,70.
armour	III,46,46.
arms	III,17,54; ,46,30.
around	III,22,5.
arouse	I,61,163.
art [are]	I,27,66; II,46,4; ,53,16; ,,49; ,63,2; ,64,3; ,65,6; ,72,8; ,,18.
art [artifice]	I,47,9; II,70,36.
as	I,21,17; ,27,50; ,,53; ,30,14; ,51,101; ,54,3; ,,5; ,60,5; ,62,18; II,3,9; ,9,15; ,16,10; ,17,27; ,49,36; ,54,33; ,58,9; ,,44; ,,69; III,17,41; ,19,20; ,25,36; ,38,13; ,,44; ,,48; ,42,64; ,43,49; ,51,11; ,59,1; ,64,14; ,74,11.
Asar	I,49,27; ,,42.
ask	II,31,1.
assuage	I,53,36.
assume	III,34,46.

13

at	I,22,25; ,27,62; ,31,12; ,49,19; ,51,42; ,62,1; ,66,6; II,22,44; ,24,66; ,,68; ,,71; III,17,3; ,27,12; ,39,78; ,41,2; ,42,85; ,45,40; ,46,28; ,51,6; ,71,16.
attack	III,42,54.
attribute	II,55,18.
aught	I,58,23; II,70,47; III,2,18.
aum	I,56,19; III,37,100.
avail	II,54,13.
availest	II,54,19.
availeth	I,23,3.
awake	II,34,9; III,34,65.
away	II,5,16.
awful	III,42,82.
axle	II,7,11.
aye	II,44,1; ,75,1.
azure	I,14,4; ,19,2.

B

babe   II,49,38.

back   III,10,37; ,46,59.

Bahlasti   III,54,1.

balanced   I,31,20.

bare   I,62,21.

bathing   I,27,22.

battle   (III,9,11); ,46,32.

Battle of Conquest   III,9,11-13.

be   I,6,1; ,10,4; ,22,48; ,23,8; ,26,17; ,,64;
            ,27,41; ,34,12; ,36,20; ,40,38; ,41,40;
            ,42,3; ,49,28; ,,43; ,50,21; ,,35; ,51,73;
            ,52,3; ,,24; ,53,29; ,,43; ,61,52; II,4,4;
            ,5,14; ,,21; ,14,4; ,21,71; ,22,36; ,,61;
            ,24,3; ,,14; ,,78; ,29,3; ,33,4; ,35,4;
            ,49,14; ,53,13; ,57,6; ,,14; ,58,8; ,,22;

,,35; ,,56; ,59,17; ,66,9; ,,26; ,,37; ,70,11;
,,19; ,,51; ,74,7; ,76,31; ,77,2; III,3,4;
,9,18; ,10,23; ,11,3; ,,71; ,,88; ,15,3; ,18,3;
,,14; ,19,17; ,21,29; ,22,12; ,25,18; ,28,4;
,29,2; ,33,1; ,34,6; ,,17; ,,99; ,39,47;
,41,9; ,42,71; ,43,29; ,44,29; ,,35; ,,45;
,46,27; ,47,4; ,,88; ,55,4; ,,15; ,64,11.

bear	II,67,3; ,70,16.
beast	III,24,37; ,34,78.
Beast	I,15,18; III,14,8; ,22,34; ,47,19; ,,40.
beasts	II,24,37.
beat	III,38,92.
beautiful	III,39,56; ,68,7.
beautifully	III,39,49.
beautious	I,26,9.
beauty	II,20,1; ,35,10.
beauty's	III,56,3.
because	I,59,15; II,12,1; ,13,3; III,20,2.
Because	II,27,27; ,28,5; ,29,2; ,30,8; ,33,3; ,54,25; III,20,7.
become	III,25,32.
bed	II,66,11.

beds	II,24,31.
been	II,2,12.
beetles	III,25,35.
before	I,5,11; ,61,23; ,,118; II,61,5; III,8,12; ,11,76; ,25,20; ,26,10; ,29,16; ,37,63; ,44,47; ,46,12.
beggar	II,58,59; ,,79.
begone	II,56,1.
behold	I,7,1; ,9,6; ,50,11; ,54,12; ,,18; ,55,8; II,5,1; ,24,1; III,73,14.
being	II,15,5.
bend	I,19,5.
bending	I,26,24.
bends	I,14,12.
Bes-na-Maut	III,38,88.
best	III,24,2.
better	I,61,6; III,29,8.
between	I,22,53.
beware	II,24,89; ,59,1; III,2,19; ,43,5.
beyond	II,51,2; III,60,5.

bid	III,38,105.
big	III,12,5.
bind	I,22,44.
black	I,26,40; ,60,31; II,5,9; ,52,8; III,39,54.
blasphemy	III,49,9.
blessed	II,53,21; III,14,7.
blessing	II,79,9; III,34,96.
blind	I,60,34; III,42,10.
blind (v)	III,52,11.
blindness	II,14,21.
bliss	III,39,94; ,62,16.
blood	I,59,13; III,11,60; ,,79; ,23,29; ,24,3; ,,12.
blue	I,14,27; ,26,30; ,60,37; ,64,4; II,50,1; III,70,17.
body	I,26,45; ,,78; ,27,25; ,32,37; II,21,75; ,62,17.
bond	I,41,25.
book	I,35,8; ,36,16; ,39,5; ,47,2.
Book	I,48,20; ,57,63; II,38,12; III,39,42; ,63,5.

Book of the Law II,38,12-15; III,39,42-45; ,63,5-8.

bosom	I,61,45.
both	I,11,7.
bottom	III,73,12.
bound	I,42,8.
bowels	I,55,5.
brass	III,30,6.
breast	III,38,90.
breathe	II,68,8; III,37,50.
breathed	I,28,2.
breed	III,27,4; ,45,13.
bride	II,2,22; ,16,12; ,50,11.
Bride	II,37,12; III,22,37.
bright	II,22,11.
brilliant	I,64,13.
bring	I,15,41; III,34,56; ,46,19.
brothers	III,58,14; ,59,2.
brows	I,18,4; ,27,15.

Buddhist	III,53,14.
burn	I,18,1; ,62,15; ,63,8; III,25,2; ,30,8.
burnest	I,61,20.
burning	II,24,101; III,40,12.
burns	II,6,6.
burnt	III,34,18.
business	III,41,14.
but	I,16,11; ,17,1; ,23,1; ,27,52; ,31,24; ,34,1; ,36,17; ,38,4; ,40,12; ,41,31; ,42,19; ,47,1; ,49,35; ,51,67; ,,111; ,53,41; ,56,46; ,57,66; ,60,35; ,61,1; ,,57; ,,97; II,9,14; ,,22; ,11,10; ,15,15; ,19,10; ,21,66; ,24,29; ,34,1; ,50,12; ,53,32; ,,51; ,58,77; ,71,1; ,76,25; III,10,32; ,13,1; ,34,1; ,39,72; ,40,1; ,42,14; ,44,1; ,47,9; ,,49; ,57,11; ,58,1; ,72,19.
buy	III,21,10.
by	I,7,5; ,22,8; ,,15; ,31,21; ,32,32; ,,38; ,,44; ,,49; ,36,26; ,47,7; ,48,18; II,5,23; ,15,12; ,24,35; ,70,29; ,,41; III,38,87; ,,93; ,39,59.

C

cakes	III,25,6.
call	I,46,12; ,,15; III,19,5.
called	I,15,23; II,27,26; III,35,8.
calling	I,62,32.
calls	I,40,2.
can	I,32,47; ,41,27; III,47,103.
cannot	II,58,80.
canst	II,59,12; ,70,14.
care	I,31,9.
caress	II,63,23.
caressed	II,24,34.
cast	II,5,15; ,58,36; III,43,44.

catch	III,16,6.
cattle	III,12,2.
centuries	II,52,40; III,34,10.
centre	I,6,6; II,3,8.
certain	II,58,75.
certainty	I,58,7.
chance	I,29,10; III,39,89; ,47,23.
change	I,36,14; ,54,1; II,54,38; ,58,5.
chant	I,62,44.
charge	I,61,113.
chaste	III,55,13.
chief	I,23,10.
child	I,55,2; ,56,18; II,39,7; III,12,8; ,24,15; ,43,36; ,45,17; ,47,90.
children	I,5,13; ,12,4; ,15,35.
choose	I,57,34; II,58,66; III,4,1.
chosen	I,15,7; ,17,6; ,31,28; ,50,42; ,57,41; II,19,20; ,25,8; ,53,19; ,65,9; ,76,28.
circle	I,60,19; ,,25; II,7,20; III,47,75.

circumfrence II,3,12.

city III,11,30.

claws III,53,3.

clear I,56,52.

clerk-house III,41,6.

close [proximity] I,40,13.

close [seal] III,10,40.

cluster III,22,17.

coiled I,61,165; II,26,6.

coiling II,26,12.

cold III,43,64.

colour I,60,29; III,10,34.

come I,12,1; ,61,38; ,,108; ,,117; ,,169; II,2,1; ,7,21; ,64,29; ,,35; ,66,47; III,10,36; ,39,11; ,62,8; ,64,3.

cometh I,22,65; ,56,16; II,76,18; III,31,2; ,47,51.

comment I,36,24; III,39,38; ,40,6; ,63,11.

company I,2,5.

compassion II,21,20; III,43,9.

complement II,2,18.

concealed I,34,17; II,59,10.

concubine III,14,13.

confounded I,52,8.

conquer III,11,10.

conqueror II,49,5.

Conquest III,9,13.

consciousness I,26,68.

console II,48,15.

consoled II,48,20.

consoler II,48,23.

consume III,38,58.

continuous I,27,35; ,,67.

continuity I,26,71.

convert III,42,39.

convey III,11,34.

Coph [Koph/Qoph?] III,72,17.

Coph Nia III,72,17-18.

core II,6,15.

count	III,19,10.
covered	I,61,125; III,44,36.
cowards	III,57,4.
cower	III,46,11.
crapulous	III,54,7.
crawl	III,43,57.
creation	I,30,4.
creeds	III,54,8.
creeping	III,25,40.
cries	II,30,5.
cross	III,51,16.
crown	II,72,24.
crushed	III,72,28.
cry	II,54,5.
cube	II,7,17.
curse	I,41,37; II,28,3; III,50,1; ,,3; ,,5.

"Curse them! Curse them! Curse them!" III,50,1-6.

curses	III,16,14.

D

damn	III,18,5.
damned	II,33,6; ,49,16.
danger	II,27,4; III,11,48.
dare	III,57,8.
dark	I,56,61.
daughter	I,64,6.
day	II,24,117; ,42,4; III,10,40; ,,42.
days	II,38,6.
dead	II,17,17; ,18,3; ,49,18.
deadlier	III,42,74.
deal	III,3,19.

death	I,51,35; ,58,14; II,6,37; ,41,19; ,45,3; ,52,27; ,63,16; ,66,21; ,,24; ,,35; ,72,21; ,73,3; ,,4; ,,9; ,,10; ,74,19; III,37,60.
deem	II,58,2; III,16,1.
deep	I,33,7; II,68,11.
defunct	III,2,14.
delicacy	II,70,42.
delicious	II,20,7.
delight	II,22,9; ,43,12; ,64,10; III,46,36.
delivered	I,44,7.
demand	I,58,22.
deny	II,22,79.
depart	I,41,21.
desert	I,61,17.
desirable	II,61,14.
desire	I,32,52; ,61,156; ,62,17; III,14,16.
desires	II,74,18.
desolation	(III,19,9).
despise	III,57,1; ,,15.

despised	III,43,53; ,55,17.
destroy	III,42,19; ,,60.
devour	II,14,14.
dew	I,27,18.
didst	III,38,10.
die	II,21,12; ,,60; ,,65; ,68,12; III,43,64.
difference	I,4,8; ,22,50.
Din	III,53,17.
dine	III,39,74.
direful	I,52,32.
disappear	I,47,13.
discover	III,47,60.
dissolution	I,30,20; II,44,12.
dissolve	II,21,79.
divide	I,25,1.
divided	I,29,4; ,41,30.
divine	III,47,42.
division	I,30,12; III,2,3.

do   I,21,11; ,22,40; ,40,6; ,,33; ,42,21; ,43,1;
              ,58,20; II,52,54; ,69,4; ,70,46; III,21,35;
              ,39,101; ,62,3.

Do what thou wilt   III,60,6-9.

does   II,30,13.

dog   II,19,8; ,33,9.

dogs   II,27,35; ,45,6.

done   II,9,21; III,41,10; ,48,8.

door   III,38,27; ,,65.

dost   II,46,1.

doth   II,27,9.

Double Wand of Power III,72,7-10.

double-wanded   III,34,44.

doubt   II,72,12.

dove   I,57,28.

down   I,26,25; II,21,27; ,26,31; ,27,22; ,52,34;
              ,58,37; III,11,85; ,23,25; ,34,19; ,42,78.

drag   III,42,77.

drawn   III,47,69.

dread   II,44,7.

dress   I,51,76.

drink [v]   I,51,86; ,63,16; II,70,27; ,,28; III,39,77.

droop   II,26,30.

dropping   III,24,17.

drugs   II,22,28.

drunk [drunken] II,22,37.

drunkenness   I,61,151; II,22,20.

dung   III,6,1.

dusk   III,43,59.

dust   I,61,63.

dwell   III,38,111.

dying   II,17,20.

E

each   III,39,63.

eagerly   III,16,4.

earnestly   I,61,115.

earth   I,21,20; ,26,41; ,53,48; ,58,6; ,61,92;
II,18,21; ,26,43; ,,48; ,58,20; III,17,32;
,,36; ,45,25.

Earth   I,40,32.

East   I,49,18; ,56,6; III,21,7.

easy   III,11,17; ,21,31; ,40,9.

eat   I,51,82; II,14,17; III,11,101; ,25,8.

eating   III,27,14.

ecstasy   I,13,9; ,14,14; ,26,86; ,53,42; ,58,18;
II,21,85; ,44,15; ,66,4.

egg II,49,40.

eight II,15,21; ,,25.

"eight and ninety rules of art" II,70,31-36.

"eight, eighty, four hundred & eighteen" I,46,17-22.

Eighties III,46,10.

elements II,36,6.

eleven II,16,9; ,,14.

11 I,60,4.

else I,41,34.

emblems I,51,33.

emphatically II,53,17.

Empress II,15,35; ,16,4.

empty III,72,24.

end I,66,8; II,79,2; III,61,4.

ending III,75,2.

enemies III,24,25; ,26,5; ,68,9.

engine III,7,7.

enginery III,6,5.

English	II,55,10; III,39,35.
enjoy	II,22,66.
enough	II,33,1; III,11,13.
enter	I,51,38.
enthroned	III,61,11.
entrap	III,42,48.
equation	I,56,41.
Equinox	I,49,21; II,40,12; III,34,37.
especial	III,21,19.
establish	III,38,33; ,41,1.
eternal	II,44,14.
Eternity	I,59,22.
even	II,56,4; III,16,16.
ever	I,16,4; ,27,42; ,52,26; ,53,49; II,21,87; ,29,6; ,58,25; ,,43; ,72,2; ,,19; ,74,22; ,76,14; III,10,27; ,39,22; ,74,17.
every	I,3,1; ,,4; ,4,1; ,44,14; II,6,8; ,,17; ,42,3; ,43,3.
everywhere	II,3,6.
evil	II,5,12.

exalt	III,22,19.
exceed	I,61,87; II,70,40; ,71,2; ,,3.
excellent	II,67,14.
exhaust	II,63,3.
exhausted	II,69,10.
existence	I,26,73; II,9,5.
Exorcist	II,7,7.
expect	I,52,30; ,56,1.
expected	I,56,14.
expiration	II,63,12.
exposure	II,22,55.
expound	II,76,23.
extended	II,2,26.
eyes	I,62,13; II,24,49; ,50,19; ,53,24; ,61,7; III,51,8.
eyesight	II,51,10.

F

face	III,52,7.
factor	II,32,10.
fade	III,10,31.
faery	I,28,7.
fail	II,46,3.
failure	III,47,79.
faint	I,28,5.
faith	I,58,9.
fall	II,27,21; ,67,8; III,20,5; ,26,9; ,34,33; ,47,105.
fallen	II,48,4; ,53,50.
Fates	III,17,9.

fear	II,22,73; ,46,8; ,53,1; ,,47; III,16,9; ,17,1; ,,5; ,,15; ,42,87.
feast	II,37,2; ,38,2; ,39,2; ,40,2; ,,9; ,41,2; ,,7; ,,11; ,,17; ,42,2; ,43,2; ,44,2.
feasts	II,36,8.
feel	I,31,15; II,18,7; ,21,18; ,69,6.
feet	I,26,52.
fell	I,33,4.
fellows	II,18,5.
fever	III,34,58.
few	I,10,5.
fierce	II,24,110.
fifth	II,49,28.
fifty	I,24,10.
fight	III,57,10; ,59,3.
fill	I,12,11; ,51,96; III,37,103; ,45,28.
filthy	II,57,12; ,,15.
find	II,24,20; ,,60; ,55,14; ,66,3.
fine	I,50,34; ,51,80.

fire	I,50,31; II,20,11; ,24,44; ,41,4; III,11,58; ,34,13; ,67,9.
first	I,56,37; II,37,5; III,3,5; ,64,6.
"Five Pointed Star"	I,60,14-16.
flame	I,16,18; ,26,28; ,61,34; ,62,35; II,6,4; III,38,11.
flaming	II,24,53.
flap	III,52,2.
flesh	III,11,99; ,53,8.
floor	I,51,9; ,,52.
flow	III,11,80.
flowers	I,26,57.
fly	III,33,4.
foam	I,51,92.
fold	I,15,38.
folk	II,17,22; III,17,21.
follow	I,32,4; II,76,19; ,,34; ,,45; III,44,10.
folly	I,36,21; II,22,51; ,54,8; III,17,22.
foods	I,51,84.

fool   I,48,5; II,59,14; III,63,2.

foolish   II,7,26.

fools   I,11,3; ,,14; ,31,3; ,57,16; II,15,14;
            III,57,14.

for   I,16,1; ,22,62; ,26,47; ,29,1; ,,5; ,,8; ,31,1;
            ,34,21; ,40,17; ,44,1; ,54,11; ,56,11;
            ,57,19; ,60,51; ,61,46; ,63,19; II,7,28;
            ,8,8; ,13,1; ,15,1; ,,29; ,,43; ,18,12; ,21,16;
            ,,86; ,,99; ,22,81; ,24,6; ,27,7; ,29,5;
            ,32,6; ,33,7; ,37,3; ,38,3; ,39,3; ,40,3;
            ,,10; ,41,3; ,,8; ,,12; ,,18; ,45,4; ,48,12;
            ,58,24; ,64,44; ,73,8; ,78,4; III,10,26;
            ,,48; ,21,32; ,22,14; ,,32; ,,41; ,23,1; ,29,9;
            ,37,20; ,39,21; ,,23; ,46,60; ,47,20; ,,100;
            ,55,8; ,56,2; ,71,11; ,72,25.

forbid   III,11,8.

forbidden   II,73,12.

force   II,20,9; ,24,92; III,17,50; ,29,14; ,45,34;
            (,72,15).

Force of Coph Nia   III,72,15-18.

forest   II,24,24.

forge   III,32,3.

forsaken   II,56,25.

forth   I,12,2; ,62,33; II,26,36.

38

forth-speaker III,37,17.

Forties   III,46,8.

fortify   III,5,1.

fortress   I,57,48.

found   II,3,15.

four (4)   I,51,3; ,,45; II,49,24.

fourfold   III,49,6.

418   II,78,47.

"4638 ABK24 ALGMOR 3Y ˣ 24 89 RPST OVA L"
             II,76,1.

foursquare   II,78,33.

fourth   III,67,3.

fresh   III,23,28; ,24,11; ,34,57.

friends   II,24,12.

from   I,32,23; ,44,8; ,56,4; ,,8; ,,12; III,11,22;
             ,24,18; ,31,6; ,32,1; ,34,59; ,43,47;
             ,45,14; ,47,106; ,73,4; ,,9.

full   III,25,33.

fullness   II,63,7.

further   II,15,47.

G

garment	II,58,68.
garments	III,44,41.
gates	I,51,41; ,,46.
gather	I,15,33; ,61,72.
gemmed	I,14,3.
get	III,10,1.
girders	III,61,17.
girt	III,11,72.
give	I,22,22; ,32,48; ,58,2; ,61,55; III,7,3; ,11,95; ,39,85.
given	I,15,30; ,20,14; ,50,22.
giver	II,6,24.
gives	I,61,59.

giveth	II,22,6.
glad	II,76,52.
gladness	II,53,31.
glass	III,10,47.
gleam	II,50,15.
globe	I,14,24.
globed	III,34,83.
glorious	III,74,10.
glory	I,15,43; ,60,50; II,22,12; ,74,12.
go	II,5,30; ,,30; ,7,33; III,46,47; ,,49.
god	III,3,11.
God	I,21,3; ,,29; ,57,56; II,19,3; ,22,77; ,23,7; III,34,76; ,36,7; ,37,54; ,61,10.
gods	III,17,11; ,37,58; ,49,12.
Gods	I,11,9; ,49,24; II,40,15; ,78,15.
gold	I,51,17; ,60,39; II,50,5; III,30,13; ,31,13; ,32,2; ,65,4.
good	II,5,19.
goodly	I,51,74.

goods	I,61,73.
grades	I,40,22.
grave	II,24,4.
Great Equinox	III,34,36-37.
greater	II,24,86; ,41,16.
green	II,50,26.
greet	III,37,36.
gross	I,50,27.
group [v]	III,22,4.
gums	I,59,8.

H

Had	I,1,1; II,64,22.
Hadit	I,6,3; ,14,21; ,21,35; II,1,5; ,2,15; ,21,89; ,79,7; III,17,42; ,38,117; ,40,11; ,45,48.
hail	II,64,15; ,,16; III,71,1.
hair	I,59,18; II,24,54.
half	I,34,13; ,,16; ,47,5; ,56,38; III,35,2.
hand	II,11,6; III,38,18; ,39,60; ,71,17; ,72,22.
hands	I,26,37.
hangs	III,51,13.
hard	II,60,3; ,62,14.
harder	II,68,1.
hardly [harshly]	III,3,20.
harlot	III,43,54.

harm	II,22,42.
hast	I,42,16; ,56,48; II,10,4; III,38,46.
hate	II,11,4; ,48,18.
hath	I,49,12; ,57,40; II,2,9; III,25,12.
have	I,20,13; ,47,3; ,50,49; ,60,47; II,8,4; ,21,2; ,56,24; III,11,47; ,38,61; ,72,27.

Hawk-headed III,34,103; (,70,4-5).

Hawk-Headed Lord of Silence & of Strength
III,70,4-11.

Hawk's head III,51,3.

he	I,16,2; ,22,27; ,36,22; ,37,23; ,38,1; ,,5; ,40,10; ,51,57; ,57,37; II.21,80; ,27,19; ,,30; ,33,5; ,57,1; ,58,70; ,59,16; ,74,13; ,76,21; III,20,9; ,42,76; ,47,104; ,51,12; ,63,13.
he	I,55,6.
head	II,26,21; ,,3; ,68,7; (III,51,3).
headdress	I,61,129.
headed	(III,34,103).
Headed	III,70,5.
hear	II,17,1.

heart	I,6,8; ,32,41; ,53,12; ,61,30; II,6,9; ,46,11; ,62,6; ,66,51; III,40,45; ,43,14; ,,41; ,44,26.
hearts	I,15,49; ,62,38; II,22,16; ,24,102; ,42,7.
Heathen	III,11,87.
heaven	I,2,7; II,76,42; III,17,28; ,24,22.
Heaven	I,21,23; ,27,38; ,33,17.
hell	I,41,45; II,60,8.
Hell's	II,63,25.
help	I,5,1; II,70,3.
her	I,16,21; ,26,35; ,,43; ,,50; ,27,13; ,,20; ,62,12; ,,42; III,43,13; ,,35; ,,40; ,,45; ,44,3; ,,9; ,,16; ,,23; ,,25; ,,28; ,,34; ,,44; ,45,5; ,,15; ,,29; ,55,9.
here	II,52,61.
hereafter	II,44,8; ,52,63.
Hermit	I,40,24.
hermits	II,24,15.
herself	III,44,5.
Heru-pa-kraath	II,8,3.
Heru-ra-ha	III,35,7.

hidden	I,54,22; III,74,8.
hide	II,53,35; ,58,81.
hiding	II,1,3; ,79,5.
Hierophant	II,18,7.
Hierophantic	I,50,9.
higher	II,51,8.
highest	I,50,46; II,19,12.
him	I,16,13; ,20,16; ,22,14; ,,23; ,23,7; ,26,23; ,51,37; ,,48; ,56,2; II,59,24; III,47,44; ,,53; ,,95; ,52,12; ,64,2; ,,13.
his	I,15,21; ,27,23; ,48,7; ,49,14; ,,51; II,28,7; ,37,11; ,58,67; ,,82; III,14,15; ,22,36; ,31,12; ,47,89.
hither	III,2,41; ,39,12.
ho	I,51,61.
hold	II,67,1; ,,2; ,68,2; III,2,20.
holier	III,48,17.
holy	III,34,3.
Holy Chosen One	II,65,8-10.
homeward	III,2,5.

honey	III,23,6.
honour	II,56,10.
Hoor	I,49,49.
Hoor-paar-kraat	I,7,10.
Hoor-pa-kraat	III,35,9.
hope	II,70,5.
host	III,24,20.
hour	I,61,69; III,14,5.
house	I,56,15; II,78,46; III,9,22; ,11,26; ,34,25.
House	I,57,54; II,2,34; III,38,68; ,,109.
how	III,38,8.
Hrumachis	III,34,39.
hungered	(III,43,66).
hurt	I,22,66; II,59,23.
hurting	I,26,53.

I

I   I,13,1; ,20,12; ,21,7; ,,21; ,22,3; ,,20; ,,31;
     ,24,1; ,26,13; ,29,2; ,32,29; ,,46; ,,51;
     ,34,6; ,46,14; ,53,18; ,58,1; ,,21; ,60,46;
     ,61,112; ,,130; ,,133; ,,143; ,63,20; ,,23;
     ,64,1; ,,9; II,2,14; ,,23; ,3,4; ,4,7; ,6,1;
     ,,19; ,7,1; ,,8; ,,31; ,8,9; ,11,1; ,,11; ,15,2;
     ,,19; ,,30; ,16,1; ,22,1; ,,30; ,23,1; ,,9;
     ,26,1; ,,17; ,,22; ,,29; ,,45; ,47,2; ,48,5;
     ,,9; ,,14; ,,17; ,49,1; ,,6; ,,35; ,50,3;
     ,52,57; ,53,33; ,,52; ,56,23; ,62,1; ,65,1;
     ,69,5; III,3,8; ,,17; ,7,1; ,11,7; ,,14; ,,93;
     ,17,46; ,21,15; ,22,21; ,37,1; ,,7; ,,14; ,,33;
     ,,35; ,,44; ,,65; ,,66; ,38,29; ,,60; ,,78; ,,91;
     ,,96; ,42,22; ,,26; ,43,31; ,,37; ,,42; ,45,3;
     ,,12; ,,26; ,46,1; ,,17; ,,25; ,47,55; ,48,10;
     ,49,1; ,51,4; ,52,1; ,53,4; ,54,3; ,70,1;
     ,72,1; ,,26.

if   I,40,9; ,41,13; ,,18; ,51,63; ,52,1; ,,6; ,,21;
     ,61,10; II,21,73; ,26,16; ,,28; ,30,1; ,31,1;
     ,59,15; ,70,25; ,,37; ,,44; ,72,6; ,,16;
     III,43,6; ,,15.

ill	,8,7; ,10,5.
ill-ordered	III,11,24-25.
image	III,21,4; ,,13.
images	III,22,3.
in	I,5,8; ,8,4; ,,10; ,13,6; ,,11; ,14,13; ,15,20; ,20,7; ,23,4; ,27,26; ,36,11; ,49,16; ,,50; ,50,16; ,,23; ,,37; ,,44; ,51,39; ,,79; ,56,50; ,,59; ,58,11; ,,24; ,60,20; ,61,15; ,,43; ,,67; ,,93; ,,99; ,,120; ,62,24; ,,41; II,3,1; ,6,7; ,,13; ,7,18; ,12,4; ,15,24; ,19,6; ,21,13; ,,83; ,24,22; ,,30; ,,47; ,,79; ,,108; ,,115; ,26,10; ,27,5; ,42,5; ,,8; ,44,16; ,46,9; ,49,39; ,50,6; ,,17; ,52,45; ,53,37; ,54,41; ,56,8; ,62,4; ,63,4; ,64,30; ,,36; ,66,5; ,,12; ,67,5; ,,10; ,70,6; ,76,39; III,10,9; ,,45; ,11,27; ,17,27; ,21,5; ,27,10; ,28,6; ,30,10; ,34,81; ,37,4; ,38,6; ,,16; ,,36; ,39,24; ,,33; ,,50; ,,92; ,40,13; ,44,6; ,,12; ,46,31; ,,51; ,47,14; ,,21; ,,34; ,,77; ,49,3; ,52,5; ,61,12; ,74,5.
incense	I,59,2; ,61,22.
indeed	II,15,33.
Indian	III,53,11.
infinite	I,4,4; ,15,12; II,32,11.
Infinite	I,22,33; ,,37.

initiating	I,49,59.
ink	III,39,18; ,,52.
innermost	I,61,154.
innocence	II,22,57.
inspired	III,37,16.
inspiration	II,63,10.
intellect	I,50,38.
intimate	III,67,8.
into	I,15,36; ,,47; ,33,5; ,40,14; II,27,23; III,38,66; ,47,6.
inviolate	III,55,3.
invisible	II,49,31; III,34,24.
invoke	I,57,1; III,37,34.
invoking	I,61,25; II,30,7.
is	I,3,6; ,4,3; ,,6; ,7,3; ,8,3; ,13,10; ,,15; ,14,5; ,15,14; ,,27; ,16,3; ,,14; ,20,6; ,21,26; ,24,7; ,30,2; ,,13; ,31,18; ,,19; ,32,27; ,34,20; ,35,5; ,39,6; ,41,5; ,,23; ,,35; ,44,13; ,46,2; ,48,3; ,49,56; ,50,2; ,51,13; ,57,7; ,,26; ,,31; ,,68; ,,74; ,59,3; ,,11; ,60,3; ,,26; ,,30; ,61,5; ,66,5; II,2,29; ,3,13; ,6,29; ,7,24; ,,30; ,9,6; ,,24; ,15,10;

„27; „45; ,16,13; ,19,1; „23; ,21,21; „34;
„41; ,22,47; „58; ,23,5; ,26,14; „39;
,27,2; ,31,6; ,32,3; „8; ,44,5; „10; ,45,2;
,46,7; ,49,21; „26; „30; ,50,16; ,51,5;
,52,2; „7; „10; „18; „29; ,57,3; „11;
,58,21; „32; „60; „73; ,59,7; ,61,2; ,63,13;
,64,11; ,69,7; ,70,2; ,72,22; ,73,11; ,74,21;
,78,6; III,2,2; „7; „13; „16; ,9,6; „81; „98;
,40,8; ,42,34; ,46,40; „44; ,47,70; „80;
,48,7; ,60,2; ,61,2; ,62,15; ,69,2; ,71,14;
,72,23; ,74,2; „16; ,75,6.

Isa	I,49,30; „46.
island	III,4,4.
it	I,7,2; ,27,40; ,32,31; ,41,41; ,42,2; ,46,13; „16; ,50,19; ,53,33; ,57,80; II,7,29; ,21,70; ,22,46; ,51,4; ,52,9; „17; ,54,17; ,58,45; „54; ,66,30; ,72,13; ,76,24; III,3,3; ,5,2; ,6,2; ,8,2; ,10,8; „21; „28; „39; „44; ,11,35; „43; ,19,15; ,21,27; ,25,17; „30; „37; ,29,6; ,34,16; ,37,102; ,38,49; ,39,25; „71; „81; „97; ,47,64; „86; „107; ,63,15; ,64,9; ,68,4.
its	II,74,11; III,19,12; ,38,9; „56; ,47,78; ,63,10; ,68,8.
itself	III,10,6.

J

jasmine	I,51,28.
jasper	I,51,21.
Jesus	III,51,10.
jewels	I,61,84; ,63,15; III,44,38.
Jews	I,46,11.
joy	I,13,14; ,,19; ,30,18; ,53,46; ,61,111; II,9,8; ,21,46; ,24,74; ,,82; ,26,15; ,35,8; ,42,10; ,66,17; ,70,18; III,45,31; ,46,24.
joyous	II,70,48; ,72,20.
joys	I,31,23; ,32,16; ,58,4.
judgments	I,52,33.
just	II,15,18.

K

Ka	III,37,86.
Kaaba	III,41,4.
keen	III,58,3.
Kephra	III,38,74.
kept	III,25,23; ,29,5.
key	I,20,2; ,46,5; III,47,72; ,,82.
Key	III,47,62.
Khabs	I,8,2; ,,12; ,9,4; II,2,28; III,37,91.
Khu	I,8,6; ,,9; III,37,80.
Kiblah	III,10,25.
kill	III,18,9; ,44,24.
kin	II,28,8.
king	II,21,53; III,34,92.

King	II,15,38; ,21,78; ,24,94; ,,96; ,58,62; ,,64; ,59,9; ,,19; ,74,24; ,,27.
kings	II,21,25; ,58,17; III,45,22.
Kings	II,58,23; ,64,46.
kinsfolk	II,18,24.
kiss	I,14,16; ,53,21; ,61,48.
kisses	II,44,18; ,62,9; ,67,15.
kissing	I,27,12.
knew	II,48,7.
knewest	II,12,8.
know	I,15,4; ,50,59; II,17,25; ,56,21; ,76,13; III,16,18; ,22,53; ,42,17.
knower	II,13,7.
knowest	I,26,59; II,76,8; III,21,25.
knoweth	I,22,28.
knowing	I,57,42.
knowledge	I,32,10; II,6,31; ,,35.
Knowledge	II,5,29; ,22,7.
known	I,10,15; ,22,5; ,34,14; II,4,5; III,2,11; ,43,30.

L

laid	III,25,19.
lambent	I,26,27.
languor	II,20,8.
lapis lazuli	I,51,18-19.
large	II,24,41.
last	I,22,26; ,36,18; III,24,34.
laugh	II,56,7; ,,13; III,42,84.
laughter	II,20,5; III,42,84.
laughterful	II,63,20.
law	I,33,32; ,46,8; ,57,9; ,,44; II,21,36; ,,43; III,60,4.
Law	I,34,19; ,35,10; ,39,5; ,40,43; II,38,15; III,9,8; ,39,45; ,,83; ,63,8.

leaping	II,20,4.
learn	I,37,25; II,2,5; ,10,8.
leave	I,56,42; III,43,17.
leavings	III,23,9.
left [spatial]	III,72,21; ,73,7.
left [remaining]	II,17,14.
length	II,74,2.
lest	II,24,90; ,59,5.
let	I,10,1; ,22,46; ,23,6; ,27,39; ,,56; ,42,1; ,49,26; ,,41; ,50,32; ,,56; ,51,36; ,,47; ,57,14; II,5,10; ,,17; ,14,2; ,,11; ,21,10; ,,69; ,35,1; ,70,49; III,3,2; ,11,68; ,,78; ,18,2; ,22,10; ,25,16; ,37,101; ,43,1; ,44,2; ,,8; ,,15; ,,22; ,,27; ,,33; ,,43; ,47,43; ,,94; ,55,1; ,,11; ,64,1.
letter	I,36,13; ,54,10.
letters	I,57,60; II,54,37; III,47,27; ,48,6.
liars	III,68,16.
lidded	I,19,3; ,64,5.
lie [lay]	I,61,42.
lie [untruth]	II,21,56; ,22,49; ,,60; ,32,5.

life	I,58,12; II,41,13; ,66,19.
Life	I,6,21; II,6,26.
lift	II,26,18; ,53,53; ,66,48; ,68,5; ,78,1; ,,16; III,45,4.
lifted	II,58,39.
light	I,9,8; ,27,21; ,28,4; ,56,53; II,14,13; ,24,46; ,50,8; ,51,7; ,61,4; ,,11; III,17,44; ,38,4; ,,53; ,,116.
Light	II,21,96.
lighten	III,37,81.
lightening	III,61,15.
like	II,78,8.
likest	III,11,42.
limbs	II,24,42.
line	III,47,68.
listen	II,75,2.
lithe	I,26,44.
little	I,26,56; ,31,16; ,53,7; ,56,34; ,61,40; III,12,3.
live	II,19,5; ,21,67.

lives	II,74,15.
loathing	I,42,10.
locked	II,10,46.
lofty	I,50,41; III,58,11.
long	II,56,15; ,73,7; ,74,16; III,29,4.
longer	III,34,98.
longing	II,74,5.
look	I,40,11; II,53,28; ,76,44.
lord	I,5,5; ,21,34.
Lord	I,49,58; III,34,105; ,37,10; ,46,5; ,70,6; ,72,4.

Lord of Silence & of Strength   III,70,6-11.

Lord of Thebes   III,37,10-12.

Lord of the Double Wand of Power   III,72,4-10.

lords	II,18,18.
lose	I,61,65.
loud	III,44,30.
love	I,12,13; ,26,48; (,29,6); ,32,19; ,41,32; ,51,100; ,57,6; ,,10; ,,18; ,,22; ,,24; ,60,54;

,61,3; ,,101; ,,131; ,62,43; ,63,4; ,,21; ,,24; II,24,97; ,59,3; ,66,46; ,70,39; ,76,36.

love-chant	I,62,43-44.
lovely	I,26,36; ,27,14; II,66,27; ,79,17.
lover	I,41,17.
Lover	I,40,27.
love's	I,29,6; III,56,6.
love-song	I,63,4-5.
low	II,24,105; ,60,5.
lurk	III,9,1.
lust	I,44,10; II,22,65; ,24,111; III,27,5; ,,9; ,34,67.
lying	II,52,36.

M

made	I,22,51; III,38,62; ,39,58.
Magician	II,7,4.
magnificent	II,24,36.
make	I,38,7; II,27,15; III,11,16; ,25,5; ,38,31; ,40,17.
makest	III,37,56.
man	I,3,2; ,40,30; ,41,8; II,6,11; ,22,64; ,73,14; ,78,40; III,31,5; ,39,64.
manifestation	I,1,3.
Manifestation	I,66,2.
mantras	I,37,3.
many	I,10,12; ,52,20.
manyhood	I,42,7.

marks	I,52,11.
Mary	III,55,2.
mask	II,53,39.
masked	II,58,50.
masses	II,24,51.
master	II,60,11.
Master	II,65,4.
matter	III,24,39.
may	I,38,6; ,50,20; II,29,1; ,58,55; ,,65.
me	I,5,2; ,21,14; ,,31; ,22,29; ,32,12; ,49,40; ,51,114; ,52,28; ,53,51; ,,53; ,57,2; ,60,55; ,61,4; ,,24; ,,26; ,,103; ,,19; ,,171; ,62,29; ,,31; ,63,7; ,,10; ,,14; ,,18; ,65,2; ,,4; II,6,33; ,7,23; ,8,6; ,12,3; ,13,9; ,15,42; ,17,2; ,,26; ,22,23; ,27,6; ,52,32; ,54,30; ,76,32; III,11,56; ,,62; ,,77; ,22,6; ,,9; ,,20; ,25,10; ,,21; ,,44; ,29,17; ,37,21; ,,96; ,,99; ,,104; ,38,7; ,,59; ,,106; ,,120; ,43,34; ,44,11; ,46,13; ,62,7.
Me	III,62,2.
meal [grain]	III,23,4.
meanest	II,54,11.

meaneth	II,76,3.
meaning	III,16,21.
means	I,51,70; ,,72.
meetest	III,39,69.
meetings	I,62,4.
men	I,5,15; ,11,5; ,,12; ,15,51; ,27,45; ,31,5; II,14,15; ,22,18; ,24,106; ,76,47; ,77,8; ,78,12; III,17,7; ,43,48; ,44,49; ,49,14.
Mentu	III,37,19; ,38,83.
mercy	III,18,1.
mere	III,68,15.
middle	I,60,22.
midnight	III,74,15.
mightier	III,45,18.
mighty	II,77,6.
million	II,24,84.
mine	I,14,29; ,61,21; II,26,32; ,72,10; III,38,55.
mingle	III,34,80.
minister	I,7,8.

miraculous	III,10,33.
misery	II,21,15.
miss	II,27,18.
mistake	I,57,17.
mix	III,23,3.
mockers	II,56,3.
modest	II,52,15.
Mohammed	III,52,9.
money	III,17,14.
Mongol	III,53,15.
monthly	III,24,8.
moon	I,16,10; III,24,7.
more	II,63,17; ,70,17; ,72,4.
moreover	III,29,1.
most	II,61,13.
mountain	II,24,28.
much	I,54,4; II,74,20.
multiply	I,25,3.

must	I,38,2; ,50,28; II,21,59; III,41,8.
my	I,5,9; ,6,4; ,,7; ,,10; ,9,7; ,10,2; ,13,8; ,,13; ,15,34; ,21,33; ,22,9; ,24,5; ,26,65; ,,77; ,31,27; ,32,2; ,,9; ,,18; ,,36; ,,39; ,36,1; ,48,1; ,53,9; ,,11; ,,14; ,57,4; ,,38; ,,62; ,,76; ,59,1; ,,17; ,60,1; ,,28; ,61,44; ,,110; ,62,3; ,,25; II,2,21; ,,33; ,15,8; ,16,11; ,22,33; ,24,11; ,25,7; ,26,11; ,,20; ,,24; ,34,4; ,42,12; ,50,10; ,,18; ,,21; ,52,51; ,53,18; ,56,9; ,58,52; ,78,20; III,9,16; ,,20; ,11,82; ,21,3; ,29,13; ,30,1; ,34,47; ,,104; ,38,17; ,,89; ,,98; ,42,31; ,43,18; ,,27; ,44,13; ,45,33; ,46,52; ,51,2; ,52,3; ,53,2; ,70,12; ,72,20; ,74,6.
mysteries	I,54,21; II,24,5; III,47,37.
mystery	I,57,51; III,48,3.
mystic	II,78,34.

N

naked	I,14,7; ,64,12.
name	I,22,10; ,,18; ,49,53; II,2,31; ,78,32; ,,43; III,11,83; ,19,13; ,74,7.
naming	III,26,3.
nations	I,61,89.
nay	I,43,8; ,45,12.
neither	III,17,6.
nemyss	III,70,13.
never	II,4,8; ,48,6.
new	II,55,15.
Nia	III,72,18.
nigh	III,71,15.
night	I,61,13; ,64,17; II,37,6; ,43,4; III,70,16.

night-blue	III,70,16-17.
night-sky	I,64,17-18.
night-stars	I,61,13-14.
nine	II,15,11.
ninety	II,70,33.
no	I,4,7; ,21,27; ,22,49; ,40,7; ,41,24; ,42,17; ,43,4; ,56,13; ,59,12; II,19,9; ,23,6; ,44,6; ,58,74; III,24,38; ,34,97; ,39,96; ,,99; ,47,39; ,60,3.
none	I,45,14; ,48,17; II,15,32; ,52,30; ,58,32; ,66,59; ,78,7; III,8,9; ,42,13.
None	I,27,53; ,28,1.
nor	I,53,38; ,56,7; ,57,13; ,58,19; II,54,1; ,76,10; III,17,8; ,,10; ,,12; ,,17; ,,23.
not	I,8,7; ,17,4; ,21,12; ,26,53; ,27,47; ,,59; ,31,10; ,34,8; ,36,10; ,41,10; ,45,10; ,48,12; ,49,38; ,50,57; ,51,58; ,52,4; ,,25; ,53,35; ,54,2; ,,17; ,56,3; ,,57; ,57,69; ,58,8; II,2,10; ,,25; ,12,9; ,15,40; ,17,24; ,18,8; ,,11; ,19,24; ,21,19; ,,51; ,,64; ,22,41; ,,74; ,24,18; ,27,10; ,47,6; ,48,2; ,,11; ,,16; ,49,8; ,52,42; ,53,2; ,,12; ,54,28; ,,40; ,56,14; ,58,3; ,,13; ,59,22; ,67,9; ,68,9; ,72,14; ,76,9; III,2,10; ,,17; ,10,30; ,11,44; ,13,2; ,16,2; ,,10; ,,19; ,17,2; ,,16; ,18,14; ,20,11; ,21,20; ,39,31; ,42,38; ,,40;

,,42; ,46,58; ,47,45; ,,57; ,,96; ,57,9; ,63,16; ,68,12.

Not   II,15,6.

nothing   I,21,9; ,22,45; ,30,15; II,21,3.

Nothing   I,46,1.

nought   II,30,14; ,54,12; III,72,32.

now   I,15,1; ,22,1; II,14,1; ,,10; ,21,68; ,24,16; ,28,1; ,64,26; ,,28; III,3,1; ,13,3; ,48,1.

nowhere   II,3,14.

Nu   II,1,1; ,2,20; ,43,6; ,44,20; ,64,19; ,76,38; III,17,37; ,45,44.

Nuit   I,1,5; ,14,10; ,22,11; ,24,3; ,27,34; ,66,4; II,21,88; ,26,25; III,38,104.

number   I,4,2; ,60,2; II,15,9; ,78,37.

numbers   I,60,8; II,75,5.

O

o	I,5,3; ,12,3; ,14,30; ,18,5; ,19,1; ,27,33; ,41,7; ,,16; ,53,23; ,54,14; II,10,1; ,21,52; ,22,63; ,25,6; ,34,3; ,39,12; ,53,3; ,61,8; ,73,13; ,76,5; ,,27; ,77,1; ,78,19; III,11,38; ,,91; ,14,6.
O	III,37,39; ,38,82; ,,103; ,,112.
obeah	I,37,7.
obey	I,32,1.
object	III,22,25.
obtain	II,55,3.
odds	III,39,100.
of	I,1,4; ,2,3; ,,6; ,5,6; ,,14; ,7,9; ,12,12; ,14,9; ,,20; ,15,11; ,,44; ,,50; ,20,3; ,23,11; ,26,7; ,,29; ,,69; ,,72; ,,76; ,27,10; ,,19; ,,31; ,,37; ,,48; ,,60; ,28,8; ,29,11; ,30,5; ,,11; ,,19; ,31,4; ,32,8; ,,17; ,,35; ,,53;

,33,16; ,35,9; ,36,6; „29; ,37,13; „19;
,39,3; ,40,31; „41; ,41,3; ,42,6; ,44,5; „11;
,46,6; ,49,22; „39; ,51,10; „14; „34; „53;
„99; ,52,34; ,53,30; „47; ,54,8; ,55,3;
,56,39; ,57,45; „52; „55; „61; ,59,4; „16;
„21; ,60,11; „42; ,61,62; „76; „90; „102;
„152; ,62,36; „39; ,64,7; „14; ,66,3;
II,1,4; ,2,19; „32; ,5,4; ,6,10; „16; „25;
„32; „36; ,7,12; ,12,2; ,14,7; ,15,41;
,17,5; „9; ,18,19; ,19,14; „25; ,20,13;
,21,24; „37; „47; „76; „102; ,22,17; „56;
„69; ,24,10; „32; „38; „52; „112; „118;
,26,41; ,27,36; ,33,2; ,36,4; „9; ,37,7;
,38,7; „10; „13; ,39,8; ,40,13; ,42,11;
,43,10; ,44,19; ,49,9; „22; ,50,9; ,52,13;
„21; „26; „31; „38; ,53,40; ,54,24; „29;
,55,8; ,58,4; „18; ,62,10; ,63,8; „24;
,64,18; „21; „24; ,66,18; „40; „43; ,67,12;
,70,35; ,72,25; ,74,3; „10; ,76,37; ,78,38;
„44; ,79,3; „6; „15; III,1,4; ,2,24; ,3,12;
„15; ,6,6; ,9,9; „12; ,10,4; ,11,87; ,14,14;
,17,19; „52; ,19,8; ,21,3; „6; ,22,26; „44;
,23,10; „15; ,24,5; „13; „21; „24; „27;
„31; „35; ,25,3; „27; „34; ,27,8; ,30,4;
,34,34; „70; „75; ,35,3; „6; ,37,11; „18;
„73; „78; „84; „89; ,38,69; „73; „76;
„115; ,39,16; „43; ,40,4; ,44,20; ,45,8;
„23; „43; ,46,6; ,47,17; „25; „63; ,48,4;
,49,13; ,51,9; ,52,8; ,53,9; ,61,5; „8; „18;
,62,12; ,63,6; ,66,5; ,67,7; ,70,7; „10;
,71,8; ,72,5; „9; „13; „16; ,74,14.

off   III,18,4.

oh   II,64,1.

oil   III,23,14; ,,19.

old   I,57,59; II,5,6; III,43,23.

olive   III,23,18.

omnipresence   I,26,75.

Ompehda   III,54,2.

on   I,51,50; ,58,5; ,61,159; II,24,26; ,,103; III,37,70; ,46,48; ,,50; ,48,14; ,54,5.

once   I,51,43.

one   I,22,56; ,26,10; ,27,36; ,36,12; ,45,7; ,48,8; ,,9; ,,10; ,49,34; ,50,17; ,,58; ,51,6; ,52,15; ,61,47; ,,60; II,15,23; ,24,98; ,26,27; ,,50; ,66,56; ,76,17; ,,29; III,21,23; ,34,45; ,47,32; ,,50.

One   I,27,51; II,65,10.

ones   I,31,29; ,50,43; II,5,13; ,,20; ,58,51; III,42,11.

only   I,32,13; ,56,29; III,11,5; ,39,32; ,42,8.

open   III,30,5; ,37,75.

or   I,33,9; ,51,41; ,52,16; ,61,138; ,,141; II,24,25; ,54,43; ,58,38; ,78,13; III,17,29;

,,33; ,24,16; ,,30; ,30,12; ,33,5; ,37,97; ,39,75; ,,95; ,42,57.

ordeal	III,62,13; ,64,7.
Ordeal x	III,42,46-47.
ordeals	I,32,7; ,33,22; ,34,5; ,38,10; ,49,6; ,50,15; III,42,2.
order	II,55,5; III,38,22.
ordered	III,11,25.
original	III,47,13.
orison	III,25,29.
other	I,21,28; ,22,60; ,43,5; ,50,62; II,58,14; ,70,7; III,17,25; ,22,2.
others	III,22,29.
our	II,18,23; ,19,19; ,21,42; ,64,9; ,,31; ,,37; ,66,10; ,,44.
out	I,32,5; III,43,46; ,53,6.
outcast	II,21,6.
over	I,9,10; II,64,13.
overcome	II,64,4.
overmuch	III,42,43.

oversee	**III,42,5.**
overthrow	**III,42,51.**
own	**II,63,26.**
Ox	**I,48,15.**

P

pain	I,30,10; ,32,25; II,17,10.
palace	I,51,7; ,,12; ,,55.
pale	I,61,137.
pall	II,52,25.
paper	III,39,20; ,,57.
particle	I,61,61.
pass	I,50,29; II,9,18.
passion	II,64,38.
paste	III,73,1.
peace	I,58,15; II,64,39.
peck	III,51,5.
pen	II,11,9; III,40,22.

penetrant	I,26,34.
people	II,17,4; ,25,5; ,34,5.
peoples	III,8,7.
perchance	II,59,6.
perfect	I,44,16; II,15,4.
Perfect	I,45,2; ,,5; ,,8.
performed	II,35,6.
perfume [n]	I,27,30; III,23,2.
perfumes [n]	I,63,11; III,25,26.
perish	II,27,32; ,49,13.
pillars	III,71,7.
pinnacles	III,45,7.
pit	II,27,25.
pity	II,48,1; III,18,8; ,42,56; ,43,7.
place	III,34,4; ,,50; ,48,18.
play	III,57,12.
pleasure	I,61,147; II,43,9.
poor	II,18,14.

position	III,47,30.
pour	III,31,11.
poured	III,34,100.
poverty	II,58,83.
power	I,15,29; III,17,26; ,27,7; ,45,9.
Power	II,31,2; ,,7; III,72,10.
powerful	III,42,28.
precious	III,66,6.
presence	III,37,38.
presently	I,61,19.
pride	I,61,96; II,24,114; III,44,7.
priest	I,15,8; ,27,3; ,33,3; ,36,5; III,24,29; ,34,84.
priestess	I,62,9.
prince-priest	I,15,16.
princes	I,36,8; ,53,32.
printed	III,39,48.
professional	III,57,5.
promise	II,66,42.

promises	III,16,8.
proof	III,10,50; ,11,6; ,42,36; ,46,42.
prophet	I,26,4; ,32,3; ,48,2; ,53,26; ,54,15; ,57,39; ,,77; II,5,25; ,10,2; ,22,34; ,53,4; ,61,9; ,64,17; ,,20; ,,23; ,76,6; ,78,21; ,79,14; III,11,39; ,34,52; ,36,4; ,38,85.
Prophet	II,37,9; ,39,10; ,,13.
prophets	I,56,26.
protect	III,42,30.
proud	II,77,4; III,58,6.
pure	I,44,2; ,61,29; II,9,7; ,21,84.
purged	II,5,22.
purple	I,61,139; ,,149; II,24,33; ,50,24; ,51,1; ,,3.
purpose	I,44,6.
push	III,38,20.
put	I,61,158.

Q

quarter	**III**,42,58.
quarters	**III**,38,39.
Queen	**I**,27,9; ,33,15.
quickly	**III**,39,103.

R

Ra   III,37,74; ,38,70.

Ra's   III,61,13.

Ra-Hoor-Khu II,64,25; III,11,51.

Ra Hoor Khuit   I,52,35.

Ra-Hoor-Khuit   I,49,11; II,21,90; III,2,25; ,37,40;
                 ,38,121; ,42,24.

Ra-Hoor-Khu-it I,36,30.

Ra Hoor KhutIII,1,5.

Ra-Hoor-Khut   III,35,11.

rain   II,62,13.

raise   III,2,21; ,44,4.

rapid   II,63,18.

rapture	II,22,72; ,26,40; ,42,13; ,64,34; ,67,7; ,70,24.
rapturous	I,63,3.
rare	I,51,26.
rays	III,38,57.
readeth	III,63,3.
ready	III,33,2.
reason	II,32,2.
Reason	II,27,37.
red	I,60,27; II,50,14; III,23,11; ,38,10; ,39,51.
redeem	I,32,21.
refine	II,70,22.
refuge	III,17,40.
refuse	I,41,9; III,42,12.
regenerate	I,53,3.
regret	II,17,12.
reign	III,34,94.
rejoice	II,19,18; ,44,3; ,64,27; ,66,53.
rejoicing	I,62,23.

remain II,21,82.

remains II,9,27; III,72,33.

remember II,9,1; ,76,26.

reproduction III,39,15.

resinous I,59,5.

rest I,58,17.

Restriction I,41,6.

result I,44,12.

reveal I,57,79; II,54,16.

revealed I,7,4; II,2,13.

revealing III,10,5.

reverence III,62,5.

reward II,52,59; III,1,3.

rich I,51,83; ,61,83; ,,128; III,23,27; ,31,4; ,44,40.

right [power] I,42,18.

right [spatial] III,73,5.

righteous II,57,4; ,,7.

rightly II,35,5.

rise	II,34,6.
ritual	I,52,23.
Ritual	II,40,6.
rituals	I,20,5; ,33,27; ,34,10; ,49,4; II,5,3; ,35,3; ,36,3.
robe	I,61,123.
rose	I,51,30.
royal	III,58,8.
rule	I,10,10; II,24,67.
rules	II,70,34.
run	III,37,92.
runes	II,27,13.

S

sacred   I,32,40; ,56,23; III,25,42.

sacrifice   I,58,25; III,12,1; ,34,86.

sad   II,18,16; ,56,20; III,15,4.

said   I,27,6; ,33,12; ,34,3; II,53,9; III,36,2;
                 ,38,51.

saith   I,26,2.

sake   I,29,7; III,55,10; ,56,4.

save   I,56,28; III,42,7.

say   I,43,7; ,50,6; ,62,10; II,59,11; III,39,7;
                 ,47,56; ,68,11.

saying   I,52,12; ,,17.

says   II,70,10.

Scarlet Concubine   III,14,12-13.

Scarlet Woman   I,15,25-26; III,43,3-4.

scents   I,51,27.

scribe   I,36,2; ,53,24.

seal   II,66,39.

seat   I,49,15; III,61,14.

second   I,56,44; III,65,3.

secret   I,6,5; ,10,7; ,14,18; ,16,17; ,20,9; ,22,17;
                ,46,4; ,49,52; ,57,75; ,60,49; ,62,26;
                II,2,7; ,15,48; ,26,4; ,39,11; III,9,21;
                ,10,11; ,22,31; ,38,26; ,,64; ,39,29, ,49,5.

secure   III,40,20.

see   I,13,17; ,21,13; II,11,2; ,24,64; ,53,44;
                III,14,3; ,45,37.

seeing   I,60,44.

seek   I,32,11; III,42,46; ,47,46; ,,97.

seem   III,68,6.

seen   I,60,41.

seeth   II,66,29.

self   II,22,53.

self-slain   III,37,27.

send	I,53,19.
sense	I,61,155; II,22,70.
serpent	I,18,7; ,57,33; III,42,67.
Serpent	I,61,33; II,26,5.
servant	I,51,65; III,42,32.
servants	I,10,3; II,21,101; ,58,53.
serve	II,58,29.
service	II,52,52.
set	III,10,7; ,21,1.
718	III,19,21.
severe	I,38,8.
shadows	II,9,16.
shall	I,10,9; ,15,3; ,,32; ,,40; ,26,16; ,,63; ,34,11; ,36,9; ,,23; ,37,24; ,40,37; ,43,6; ,53,2; ,,34; ,55,7; ,,78; ,61,64; ,,71; ,,81; ,,86; ,,106; ,62,7; ,,14; II,4,3; ,5,27; ,19,17; ,21,81; ,22,40; ,,78; ,24,58; ,,63; ,,77; ,27,14; ,,20; ,,31; ,53,46; ,54,2; ,,15; ,56,12; ,57,5; ,,13; ,58,7; ,,21; ,,28; ,,34; ,66,25; ,,31; ,,36; ,74,6; ,76,22; ,78,24; ,,29; III,3,18; ,8,4; ,,10; ,9,15; ,10,22; ,,29; ,,35; ,11,2; ,14,2; ,15,2; ,19,4; ,,16; ,21,28; ,22,16; ,25,31; ,26,8; ,27,3; ,28,3; ,31,10;

,34,5; ,,29; ,,40; ,,53; ,,64; ,,79; ,,87; ,,93; ,38,30; ,39,46; ,,88; ,40,16; ,43,26; ,,55; ,45,35; ,,46; ,46,35; ,,56; ,47,3; ,,41; ,,59; ,,87; ,68,5.

shalt
I,54,16; ,61,37; II,21,63; ,53,11; ,,27; ,55,2; ,,13; ,73,6; ,76,11; III,11,32; ,,46; ,21,9; ,22,52; ,42,4; ,,16.

shameless
III,44,46.

shape
III,47,24.

shattered
III,34,21.

she
I,14,11; ,16,8; ,26,21; ,34,2; ,41,14; ,62,19; II,3,10; ,4,2; III,43,16; ,,56; ,45,36; ,,45.

shed
I,9,9.

sheets
III,73,3.

shoot
II,26,35.

show
III,21,17; ,38,100.

showed
III,37,43.

shrine
II,14,9.

shrinking
III,43,51.

shrouds
III,70,14.

sighing
II,17,6.

Sight	II,21,95.
sign	I,26,19; ,,62.
signs	I,49,10.
silence	(III,70,8).
silver	I,51,15; III,30,11; ,64,15.
Sin	I,14,4.
since	I,22,30; ,27,64.
sing	I,63,1.
single	I,61,122.
sink	I,51,59; ,,66.
sister	I,53,10.
six	I,24,8.
six and fifty	I,24,8-10.
sixty-one	I,46,9.
skew-wise	II,32,19.
skies	III,34,61.
sky	I,64,18; III,37,25; ,70,18.
slave	I,26,6.

slaves	II,49,11; ,54,23; ,58,27.
slay	III,26,2; ,43,33; ,46,38.
smelling	I,27,29.
smite	III,8,5; ,33,7.
smooth	III,23,24.
snake	III,38,114.
Snake	II,21,107; ,22,4; III,34,72.
so	I,17,5; ,26,20; ,32,28; ,42,11; ,47,10; ,61,105; II,59,13; ,68,10; III,38,1; ,68,13.
soft	I,26,51.
soften	III,23,22.
soldiers	III,57,6.
solve	I,56,35.
some	I,56,55; III,24,36.
son	III,74,19.
song	I,63,5; III,37,6.
sorrow	II,52,22; ,53,41.
sorroweth	II,19,22.
sorrows	II,9,12; ,17,8.

sorry	II,46,6; ,53,14.
soul	III,34,74; ,61,20.
souls	III,42,80.
space	I,15,13.
Space	I,22,34; ,27,11.
space-marks	I,52,10-11.
spangles	II,50,22.
spare	III,18,12.
sparks	III,67,5.
speak	I,27,46; ,,58.
spears	III,11,67.
spectre	II,62,37.
spell	III,2,23; ,38,99.
spelling	III,2,12.
spells	I,37,5; II,70,8.
sphere	II,3,3.
spices	I,61,79.
spit	III,42,88; ,54,4.

splendour   I,14,8; ,49,55; ,61,94; ,,166; II,64,32;
               III,74,4.

splendrous   I,18,6.

spring   II,26,9.

squared   III,47,76.

stain   III,34,88.

stamp   II,21,26.

stand   I,51,49; III,8,11; ,34,30.

standeth   III,34,27.

stands   I,62,20.

star   I,3,8; ,50,50; ,,52; II,6,18.

Star   I,57,71; ,60,16; II,21,104; ,79,18.

star-lit   II,76,41.

starlight   I,16,24.

starry   I,14,26.

stars   I,12,7; ,15,46; ,28,10; ,57,5; II,62,12;
               ,78,27.

Stars   I,22,38.

star-splendour   III,38,102.

state   I,42,5.

stature   II,78,23.

steel   III,32,4.

stele   III,10,3; ,19,2.

stele of revealing III,10,3-5.

still   II,57,8; ,,16; III,37,98.

stir   II,22,14; III,37,95.

stones   III,66,4.

stooping   I,16,23.

stops   II,30,3; ,,11.

stops [character spacing]   II,54,32.

store   I,61,75.

strange   II,22,27.

strangely   III,47,93.

streets   III,43,61.

strength   II,20,3; ,74,9; III,17,49; ,46,53; ,70,11.

Strength   II,21,93.

strike   II,60,2; III,42,70; ,45,39.

strive	II,72,1.
strong	II,21,39; ,22,62; ,70,12; III,28,5.
stronger	II,11,13.
style	I,54,7; II,54,42.
subtlety	II,70,52.
success	III,42,33; ,46,39; ,69,3.
suddenly	III,21,30.
sufferer	I,49,48.
sun	I,16,6; III,74,13.
Sun	II,21,92.
Sunset	I,64,8.
Supreme Ritual	II,40,5-6.
support	III,22,8.
supreme	III,37,51.
surpass	II,78,25.
swear	I,32,30.
sweat	I,27,32.
sweet	I,27,28; ,51,87; II,64,42.

sweeter	II,63,14.
sweetnesses	III,43,24.
swell	III,29,11.
swift	III,40,18; ,42,63.
swoon	I,33,10; II,67,11.
sword	I,37,21; III,11,75; ,34,15; ,38,15.
swords	III,11,64.
symbols	II,55,16.
system	I,50,53; ,,55.

T

Tahuti	**II**,39,4.
take	**I**,12,9; ,51,94; **II**,22,24.
taken	**I**,49,13.
talk	**III**,42,41.
Ta-Nech	**III**,38,95.
task	**I**,50,10.
teach	**I**,37,27; ,38,3.
tear [rip]	**II**,52,33; **III**,53,5.
tell	**II**,22,32; ,76,49.
temple	**I**,62,27; **III**,10,12; ,,15.
tenderness	**III**,43,11.
terrible	**III**,37,53.
test	**II**,58,76.

than	I,21,30; ,61,7; II,24,87; ,51,9; ,63,15; „21; III,42,75; ,45,19.
that	I,11,4; ,15,5; ,27,44; ,30,8; ,35,2; ,41,26; ,42,4; ,43,2; ,47,11; ,51,11; „91; ,56,17; „30; ,60,53; ,61,68; II,2,8; ,6,5; ,7,32; ,9,4; „9; „25; ,17,23; ,21,55; „57; ,22,5; „75; ,49,12; ,52,5; „35; ,53,25; „43; ,54,9; ,56,22; ,57,2; „10; ,58,33; „57; ,74,14; III,3,7; ,10,14; ,11,11; ,14,4; ,19,1; ,20,8; ,38,2; „28; ,39,67; ,40,7; ,42,45; ,47,38; „92.
the	I,1,2; ,2,1; „4; ,5,12; ,7,7; ,8,1; „5; „8; „11; ,9,3; ,10,11; „14; ,12,6; ,14,2; „6; „17; „22; „25; ,15,6; „15; „17; „24; „42; „45; „48; ,16,15; „22; ,20,1; „4; „8; ,21,2; „5; „19; ,22,36; ,23,9; ,26,3; „8; „18; „39; „55; „61; „67; „70; „74; ,27,2; „8; „17; ,28,3; „9; ,29,9; ,30,3; „6; „9; „17; ,32,6; „15; „33; ,33,2; „14; „21; „26; „31; ,34,4; „9; „18; „29; „39; „42; ,41,1; „29; „43; ,44,9; ,45,1; „4; ,46,10; ,47,4; ,48,14; „19; ,49,17; „20; „23; „44; „47; „57; ,50,8; „26; „33; „40; „45; „61; ,51,8; „32; „44; „51; „53; ,52,9; „22; „31; ,53,4; „6; „31; ,54,6; ,55,1; ,56,5; „9; „36; „40; „43; „51; „60; ,57,8; „15; „27; „32; „43; „46; „49; „53; „70; „82; ,59,19; ,60,13; „21; „24; „33; „36; „43; ,61,12; „16; „32; „88; „91; „100; „153; „160; „164; ,62,8; „34; „37; ,63,2; ,64,3; „11; „15; ,66,1; II,1,2; ,2,6; „17; „30; ,3,2; „7; „11; ,5,2; „5; „11; „18; „24; ,6,3; „14; „23; „30;

,,34; ,7,3; ,,6; ,,10; ,,13; ,,16; ,,19; ,8,11;
,9,11; ,11,5; ,,8; ,13,6; ,14,12; ,15,13; ,,17;
,,34; ,,37; ,16,3; ,,6; ,17,7; ,,16; ,,19; ,,21;
,18,13; ,,17; ,,20; ,19,11; ,21,5; ,,8; ,,22;
,,28; ,,31; ,,35; ,,38; ,,45; ,,48; ,,74; ,,77;
,,91; ,,100; ,,103; ,,106; ,22,3; ,,15; ,,54;
,24,23; ,,27; ,,73; ,,104; ,,109; ,,116; ,25,4;
,26,3; ,,42; ,,47; ,27,24; ,,34; ,35,2; ,36,5;
,,10; ,37,4; ,,8; ,38,4; ,,8; ,,11; ,,14; ,39,6;
,,9; ,40,4; ,,11; ,,14; ,42,9; ,43,8; ,44,11;
,,17; ,45,5; ,48,3; ,,19; ,,22; ,49,10; ,,23;
,50,7; ,,13; ,51,6; ,52,11; ,,14; ,,19; ,,24;
,,39; ,53,23; ,54,22; ,,31; ,,36; ,55,4; ,,9;
,58,16; ,,19; ,,26; ,62,8; ,,11; ,63,5; ,,9;
,,11; ,64,45; ,65,3; ,,7; ,66,16; ,,38; ,,41;
,67,13; ,69,8; ,70,30; ,72,23; ,74,1; ,,8;
,,23; ,,26; ,75,4; ,,7; ,76,35; ,,40; ,78,26;
,,36; ,,39; ,,42; ,79,1; ,,4; ,,13; ,,16; III,1,2;
,2,22; ,8,6; ,9,7; ,,10; ,10,2; ,,52; ,11,20;
,,23; ,,28; ,,69; ,,86; ,14,11; ,16,7; ,,13;
,17,20; ,,31; ,,35; ,,48; ,19,6; ,20,4; ,21,6;
,,22; ,22,1; ,,23; ,,28; ,,33; ,,42; ,,45;
,24,1; ,,6; ,,10; ,,19; ,,28; ,,32; ,27,13;
,31,7; ,34,9; ,,32; ,,35; ,,43; ,,60; ,,66; ,,71;
,,82; ,,89; ,,102; ,35,1; ,,4; ,36,3; ,,6; ,37,5;
,,9; ,,15; ,,23; ,,26; ,,46; ,,57; ,,71; ,,76;
,,79; ,,82; ,,85; ,,87; ,,90; ,38,38; ,,42;
,,52; ,,67; ,,84; ,39,27; ,,34; ,,41; ,,44; ,,82;
,40,2; ,,5; ,42,1; ,,9; ,,20; ,43,2; ,44,18;
,45,21; ,,24; ,,41; ,46,3; ,,9; ,,9; ,47,12;
,,15; ,,18; ,,22; ,,26; ,,61; ,48,5; ,,16; ,49,8;
,51,7; ,,15; ,52,6; ,53,7; ,,10; ,,13; ,58,2;
,,5; ,,7; ,,10; ,61,6; ,,9; ,,16; ,,20; ,63,1; ,,7;
,64,5; ,65,2; ,66,2; ,67,2; ,,7; ,70,3; ,,15;

,71,6; „9; ,72,3; „6; „11; „14; ,73,2;
,74,12; „18; ,75,1; „4; „7.

Theban	III,38,80.
Thebes	I,5,7; III,37,12.
thee	I,27,61; ,53,37; „40; II,11,3; ,22,80; ,53,36; „45; „54; ,64,8; „14; ,73,16; ,76,20; ,78,10; III,11,54; ,21,11; „18; „33; ,31,15; ,37,3; „68; ,42,49; „52.
Thee	I,27,49; II,12,5; III,37,64.
their	I,11,8; „11; ,15,37; ,18,3; ,31,7; ,60,7; II,21,14; ,24,48; ,32,16; ,54,7; III,11,98; ,42,79; „86; ,47,29.
[thelema]	I,39,7.
Thelemites	I,40,4.
them	I,19,7; ,27,57; ,55,9; ,60,52; II,14,18; ,21,11; ,24,21; „56; „61; „65; „80; ,48,8; „13; ,54,39; ,55,19; ,60,10; ,76,50; III,3,22; „9,4; ,11,90; ,18,6; „16; ,39,79; ,42,44; „53; „61; „90; ,50,2; „4; „6.
then	I,9,2; ,26,1; ,27,1; ,32,14; ,33,1; ,52,29; ,61,51; II,5,26; ,26,38; ,30,9; ,31,5; ,56,16; III,23,13; ,24,9; „23; „26; ,36,1; ,39,86; ,43,25; ,45,1; „10; ,47,66; „73; ,73,13.

there	I,4,5; ,21,25; ,22,47; ,,64; ,36,19; ,40,18; ,41,22; ,50,1; ,,12; ,51,1; ,,23; ,,68; ,57,20; ,,25; ,,30; ,59,10; II,9,23; ,14,3; ,15,44; ,23,4; ,24,7; ,,57; ,,76; ,26,13; ,27,1; ,,29; ,32,7; ,36,1; ,44,4; ,,9; ,45,1; ,49,25; ,52,1; ,58,30; ,,48; ,,72; ,61,1; ,70,1; ,,13; ,,50; ,76,15; ,78,5; III,2,1; ,,6; ,20,12; ,31,1; ,34,26; ,38,23; ,60,1; ,61,1; ,69,1; ,74,1.
thereby	I,22,63; III,47,101.
therefore	I,22,2; ,51,75; II,6,28; ,58,15; ,59,2; ,60,1.
therein	I,40,20; ,54,23; ,59,14; ,61,35; II,49,33; ,70,53.
thereof	I,22,39; II,22,38; III,15,5; ,27,15.
thereon	III,30,9.
thereupon	I,36,25.
these	I,11,1; ,31,2; ,37,22; ,54,20; ,57,58; II,18,1; ,,4; ,21,97; ,24,2; ,27,12; ,47,4; ,52,48; ,53,6; III,26,1; ,27,2; ,38,40; ,47,35.
they	I,10,8; ,15,31; ,,39; ,21,10; ,,15; ,31,14; ,47,2; ,48,13; ,49,36; ,52,13; ,,18; ,56,31; II,9,17; ,18,6; ,19,16; ,21,17; ,22,39; ,49,15; ,53,42; ,54,3; ,,20; ,,26; ,78,28; III,19,3; ,22,15; ,,39; ,26,7; ,29,3; ,,10; ,39,87.

thick	III,23,8; ,25,24.
thine	I,47,8; ,53,44; II,46,10; ,61,6; ,62,5; ,66,50; ,68,6; III,38,108.
thing	I,22,57; ,,61.
things	I,61,9; II,22,68; III,25,41.
think	II,21,50; ,24,17.
third	III,66,3.
this	I,23,5; ,30,1; ,32,26; ,35,1; ,36,15; ,46,7; ,52,2; ,53,1; ,,20; ,57,72; II,5,28; ,10,9; ,14,8; ,21,33; ,,40; ,22,50; ,,82; ,24,88; ,49,20; ,52,28; ,76,4; ,,51; III,9,5; ,11,1; ,16,20; ,21,36; ,22,50; ,25,1; ,,4; ,,11; ,39,2; ,,17; ,,40; ,,93; ,,102; ,47,1; ,,67; ,,74; ,,99; ,48,2; ,63,4.
thou	I,6,2; ,26,58; ,27,65; ,31,11; ,35,3; ,40,35; ,41,19; ,42,15; ,53,28; ,54,13; ,56,47; ,61,18; ,,36; ,,50; II,10,3; ,12,7; ,13,4; ,21,58; ,,62; ,46,2; ,,5; ,53,10; ,,15; ,,26; ,,48; ,54,10; ,,14; ,,18; ,,34; ,55,1; ,,12; ,59,20; ,63,1; ,64,2; ,65,5; ,70,15; ,,26; ,,38; ,,45; ,72,7; ,,17; ,73,5; ,76,7; ,,12; ,77,3; III,11,31; ,,41; ,,45; ,14,10; ,21,8; ,,24; ,22,51; ,38,45; ,39,9; ,,68; ,42,3; ,,15; ,,72; ,60,8.
though	I,53,27; ,56,56; II,56,5; III,11,40; ,34,11.
three	I,50,14; ,,24; III,38,5.

threefold   I,35,7.

Three Grades I,40,21-22.

thrill   II,66,14.

throne   III,34,48; ,37,72.

through   I,50,30; III,37,93; ,43,58; ;62,10; ,64,4;
                ,65,1; ,66,1; ,67,1.

throughout   III,34,8.

thus   I,22,43; ,27,43; ,50,47; II,16,8; III,9,14.

thy   I,41,11; ,42,13; ,,22; ,51,64; ,55,4;
                II,62,16; ,66,23; ,,34; ,67,6; ,70,23; ,74,4;
                ,78,22; ,,31; ,,45; III,10,10; ,37,40; ,38,4;
                ,,21; ,,34; ,,80; ,,101; ,39,37; ,40,14; ,,21;
                ,41,3; ,42,35.

Thy   III,37,49.

thyself   II,68,4; ,78,3; ,,18; III,11,33; ,42,6.

time   II,5,7; III,71,13.

times [eras]   II,36,11.

times [multiplication]   II,24,85.

to   I,13,16; ,14,15; ,16,12; ,,20; ,22,6; ,,13;
                ,41,42; ,42,20; ,50,5; ,51,5; ,53,50; ,,52;
                ,57,81; ,60,32; ,61,2; ,,41; ,,54; ,,109;
                ,,116; ,,135; ,62,28; ,,30; ,63,9; ,,13; ,,17;
                ,65,1; ,,3; II,10,7; ,17,15; ,19,4; ,22,21;

,24,19; ,26,8; ,55,17; ,60,7; ,72,3; ,75,3;
,76,18; ,,30; ,,33; ,,43; ,,48; ,79,12;
III,10,38; ,,51; ,11,18; ,,81; ,,100; ,16,5;
,,11; ,19,18; ,21,34; ,22,7; ,,18; ,33,3; ,,6;
,37,61; ,,94; ,38,19; ,,32; ,,110; ,39,62;
,,73; ,,76; ,,90; ,42,39; ,,47; ,,50; ,,81;
,45,6; ,46,21; ,,37; ,47,31; ,,47; ,48,12;
,,15; ,62,1; ,,6; ,64,12; ,68,2; ,73,6; ,,11.

To   III,34,101.

To me! To me!   I,53,50-53; ,62,28-31; ,65,1-4.

tomb   III,34,90.

tongue   I,6,11; ,32,43; ,53,15.

tongues   III,47,8.

too   III,16,3.

top   III,73,10.

torment   III,42,83.

torn   III,55,5.

torture   III,18,11.

touching   I,26,32.

toy [v]   III,43,21.

traitors   III,42,21.

trample   II,24,107; III,11,84.

trance	I,33,8.
translated	III,47,5.
trees	I,59,20.
tremble	III,37,62.
tribulation	III,62,11.
tried	I,50,36.
trodden	III,42,66.
trouble	III,11,50.
true	I,56,27.
truly	II,72,9.
truth	III,37,52.
try	III,47,48.
[tsaddeh]	I,57,67.
Tum	III,38,72.
turn	I,51,40; III,42,68; ,46,57.
twin	III,71,3.
two	I,28,12; ,45,11.

U

ultimate   III,67,4.

unassuaged   I,44,4.

unattacked   I,56,45.

under   I,12,5; ,57,3; ,,11; ,61,11; III,17,34.

undergo   III,16,12.

understand   I,25,5; ,56,32; II,27,11.

understandeth   III,63,14.

understood   II,21,72; III,3,6.

undesired   II,61,12.

unfit   II,21,9.

unimaginable   I,58,3.

union   I,29,12.

unique	II,49,3.
unite	I,41,28; ,47,6.
unity	III,37,41.
Universe	III,72,30.
unknown	II,32,13.
unlike	III,21,21.
until	III,34,31.
unto	I,20,15; ,27,7; ,33,13; ,,19; ,,24; ,,29; ,51,113; ,52,27; ,53,16; ,61,170; ,63,6; II,7,22; ,43,5; ,55,20; ,73,15; ,78,9; III,25,9; ,,42; ,36,5.
untouched	III,34,7.
unutterable	I,58,16.
unveiling	I,2,2; ,5,10.
unveils	III,37,22.
up	II,14,19; ,26,19; ,34,7; ,53,54; ,58,40; ,66,49; ,67,4; ,68,3; ,78,2; ,,17; III,21,2.
uplifted	II,62,3.
upon	I,18,2; ,19,6; ,21,18; ,26,38; ,58,13; II,21,54; ,28,4; ,53,29; ,62,15; ,64,8; ,76,46; III,9,3; ,11,89; ,17,30; ,18,15; ,31,14; ,39,39; ,,55; ,42,89; ,51,14; ,55,6.

us	**I**,33,20; ,,25; ,,30; ,40,3; ,60,12; **II**,19,15; ,,26; ,20,14.
use	**III**,25,15.
utterly	**III**,42,62; ,55,16.
uttermost	**II**,43,11; **III**,37,42.

V

value	II,54,44; ,55,7.
vault	I,32,34.
veil	II,52,4; ,,6; ,,12; ,,20; ,,41.
veiled	I,61,140; III,37,24.
veiling	II,14,6.
vengeance	III,43,28.
Vengeance	III,3,16.
venom	II,26,37.
verily	II,21,61.
vice	II,21,23.
vices	II,52,44; ,,49.
victorious	II,24,89.

Victorious City   **III**,11,29-30.

victory   **III**,46,22.

vigorous   **III**,17,51.

virtuous   **II**,52,46.

visible   **III**,22,24.

visit   **III**,43,12.

vital   **II**,15,28.

voluptuous   **I**,61,142; ,64,18; **II**,63,6.

W

wand	I,37,15; (III,72,8); ,,12.
wanga	I,37,10.
want	III,48,11.
war	III,6,7; ,28,7.
war-engine	III,7,6-7.
War	III,3,13.
warrior	I,5,4; ,51,62; III,11,92; ,46,4.
warriors	III,71,4.
was	II,58,46.
wast	II,13,5.
water	II,41,9; III,66,7.
way	I,44,15; III,38,35; ,41,15; ,44,14.

ways	I,50,25; III,37,77; ,,83; ,,88.
we	II,18,9; ,21,1; ,64,5; ,66,54; ,,57.
weak	I,31,22; II,21,32.
weakness	II,31,8.
wear	I,61,82; ,63,12.
weave	III,39,97.
well	I,50,60; ,57,36; II,52,55; III,19,11; ,41,11.
were	III,25,38; ,39,70.
West	I,56,10; III,31,8.
wet	III,43,60.
what	I,26,15; ,31,17; ,40,34; II,69,3; ,76,2; III,22,48; ,24,40; ,60,7.
wheel	II,7,14.
wheels	III,55,7.
when	I,22,24; ,51,104; II,53,5; ,56,17; III,34,38.
whence	III,47,54.
where	I,51,105; II,23,8; ,47,1.
whereof	II,22,29.

which	I,20,11; ,22,18; II,9,26; ,12,6; ,15,26; III,21,14; ,62,14.
while	I,58,10.
who	I,26,11; ,40,1; ,49,31; ,60,9; ,61,144; II,8,1; ,19,21; ,24,13; ,27,8; ,49,29; ,54,4; III,18,7; ,31,9; ,37,55; ,47,58; ,57,7; ,68,10.
whole	I,27,24; ,40,40.
whom	I,51,108; ,53,17.
whose	III,37,29.
whoso	I,23,2; ,61,58; II,66,28.
why	II,13,2; ,31,4; III,20,1.
Why	II,30,6.
wickedness	III,44,21.
wife	I,41,12.
will [do; shall]	I,22,21; ,32,20; ,40,5; ,51,103; II,22,31; ,52,58; ,53,34; ,58,71; III,7,2; ,11,15; ,,94; ,21,16; ,43,32; ,,38; ,,43; ,45,2; ,,11; ,,27; ,46,18; ,,26; ,64,10.
will [force; Will]	I,41,15; ,42,23; ,44,3; ,51,98; ,,110; ,57,12; II,10,6.
will [interrogative]	I,51,56.

Will	II,30,2; ,,10.
willing	I,61,53.
wilt	I,40,36; ,41,20; ,61,49; II,54,35; III,60,9.
wine	II,22,25; III,52,4.
winners	III,22,43.
wisdom	I,36,28; II,70,9.
wise	I,57,83; III,38,94.
with	I,21,1; ,42,12; ,48,6; ,49,29; ,51,107; ,60,17; ,61,27; ,,126; ,62,5; ,,16; II,14,20; ,15,16; ,21,4; ,22,19; ,24,40; ,,100; ,27,33; ,35,7; ,53,30; ,60,9; ,66,15; III,3,21; ,6,4; ,8,1; ,11,36; ,,53; ,,57; ,,63; ,,66; ,,73; ,23,26; ,25,25; ,29,12; ,34,12; ,38,119; ,41,13; ,43,22; ,44,37; ,45,30; ,,32; ,47,11; ,51,1; ,53,1.
withdrew	III,9,2.
within	I,61,167; III,38,107.
without	III,42,55.
woes	I,31,8.
woman	I,3,5; ,15,22; (,15,26); ,19,4; II,52,16; III,11,70; ,34,63; ,39,66; (,43,4).
women	I,61,77; II,24,39; III,55,14.

wonderful	II,78,35.
wood	I,59,6.
word	I,20,10; ,24,6; ,39,2; ,40,16; ,41,2; ,50,4; II,7,27; ,69,9; ,76,53; III,2,9; ,35,5; ,39,28; ,49,7; ,61,7.
Word	III,75,8.
words	I,49,8; ,56,21; II,32,17; ,52,47; ,53,7; ,64,43; ,75,8; III,37,30; ,75,5.
work	I,37,12; ,,18; II,66,7; III,30,7; ,40,3; ,43,19; ,44,17; ,,19.
working	II,66,13.
world	I,30,7; ,53,5; ,,8; II,21,49; III,10,53; ,71,10.
worm	II,63,27.
worship	I,9,1; II,22,22; ,78,30; ,79,11; III,9,17; ,11,37; ,,55; ,,61; ,22,27; ,34,69; ,45,42.
worshipped	II,8,2; ,,5; III,22,13.
worshipper	II,8,12.
worshippers	III,24,33.
wrath	II,24,120.
wretched	II,21,29.

write   I,33,18; ,,23; ,,28; ,34,7; II,64,41; ,66,1.

writest   I,35,4.

writing   II,10,10; ,38,9; ,66,6; III,47,16.

written   III,38,47.

wrong   I,40,8.

X

x   III,22,47.

Y

ye   I,15,21; ,17,2; ,22,7; ,,41; ,31,25; ,32,22;
,,53; ,50,48; ,51,77; ,,102; ,,109; ,52,7;
,57,35; ,61,70; ,,80; ,,85; ,,107; II,2,3; ,9,3;
,17,3; ,22,43; ,24,62; ,25,1; ,34,2; ,52,53;
,56,2; ,,6; ,,11; ,,18; ,58,6; ,,10; III,4,2;
,8,3; ,14,1; ,15,1; ,16,15; ,,17; ,28,2;
,46,34; ,,55; ,58,12; ,59,4; ,62,4; ,,9; ,71,2.

yes   II,58,1.

yearn   I,61,134.

yet   II,2,11; ,4,1; ,6,27; ,17,28; ,58,47;
III,34,22; ,42,73; ,68,1.

yonder   II,58,58.

you   I,9,11; ,13,4; ,,7; ,22,53; ,61,114; ,,132;
,,136; ,,157; ,,168; ,62,6; ,63,21; ,,25;
II,52,60; ,56,26; ,59,12; III,7,4; ,8,13;
,11,19; ,,96; ,19,19; ,26,11; ,27,11; ,46,20;
,55,19.

your   I,12,10; ,13,18; ,51,95; II,24,113; ,,119;
            ,42,6; ,52,43; III,10,24; ,11,4; ,17,39; ,,43;
            ,,53; ,25,28; ,26,4; ,34,2; ,46,29; ,,41;
            ,,45; ,54,6; ,71,12.

yours   I,13,12.

www.ingramcontent.com/pod-product-compliance
Lightning Source LLC
Chambersburg PA
CBHW060438090426
42733CB00011B/2319